Islam for today

Angela Wood

OXFORD
UNIVERSITY PRESS

About the series

We live in a world where there are people of many different religions. In many of our towns and cities Buddhists, Christians, and Jews live alongside Muslims, Hindus, and Sikhs. If you travel abroad you will soon experience whole countries that have been shaped by religion.

We all have different ways of looking at things. It could be said that we all see the world through our own "spectacles". These spectacles are made up of our beliefs, opinions, attitudes, and values. What is important to you might not be important to me.

Religious people see the world through their spectacles, and this affects the way they see and live in the world. We can't understand someone else's world view unless we look through their spectacles. The *Religion for Today* series helps you to do this by giving you the skills and knowledge to understand people with beliefs different from your own.

In learning about another religion you will also be given the chance to think about your own life. So you will not only learn *about* the religions you study; you will also learn *from* the religions.

Chris Wright, Series Editor

About this book

Muslims believe that Islam is as old as humanity, though the Islamic community began in Arabia in 622. Today there are Muslim communities in every part of the world, in almost every country, and Islam is the fastest-growing religion. The largest populations of Muslims are in the Middle East, North and West Africa, the Indian sub-continent, and South-east Asia.

Islam is about having certain beliefs and values, and performing certain actions, including rituals. But it is more than that. It is a system of law and obedience to Allah (God) – a religion that affects a Muslim's whole life. People can be Muslim whatever their nationality or background. Islam can adapt to any culture. In some places and times there are Muslim customs that are not followed in other places and times; but the essentials are found everywhere. They have not changed and will never change.

This book explores Islam through traditional writings and the words of modern Muslims.

Angela Wood

In memory of Sarah and Hagar,
and the story they shared

Practical notes

▶ Many of the words and names that Muslims use are in Arabic. In English books about Islam, Islamic terms are written with English letters and this is a guide to pronouncing them. Sometimes there are different English spellings of an Arabic word. In this book, Islamic terms are explained where they are first used and also appear in the Glossary on page 62.

▶ Some dates appear in this book. Muslims have their own dating system but also use the more common dating system for everyday life. Instead of AD they use CE (Common Era) and instead of BC they use BCE (Before the

Common Era). The Islamic dating system begins with the start of the Islamic community in Madinah in 622 CE. An Islamic year is made up of twelve lunar months, each lasting 29 or 30 days, making about 354 days.

▶ It is impossible to create a drawing, painting, sculpture, or model of Allah (God) as Allah is a Spirit and has no body. It would be making an idol, not a true image of Allah. Making and worshipping idols is forbidden in Islam. The Prophets and Caliphs were highly respected human beings. Muslims generally do not depict them because they would easily become idols.

Contents

ONE

Who are Muslims? What is Islam?

In this unit you will find out about the meanings of "Islam" and "Muslim".

"Assalamu aleikum!" That's how Muslims greet each other all over the world, whatever language they normally speak. The words are Arabic for "Peace be upon you!"

The reply is always, "Wa aleikum salam!" (meaning "Upon you be peace!"). Sometimes, it's just "Salam" ("Peace!"), for short.

Arabic words have a "root" of letters, and words with the same root have similar meanings. "Salam" (peace), "Islam", and "Muslim" all have the root S-L-M. Muslims understand that real peace is not just between people but within a person, and that such "peace within" comes when they give themselves to Allah. Islam is the religion of submission (giving oneself) to Allah; its followers are called Muslims.

The Muslim community

All the people in the photographs here are Muslim. Muslims come from all nationalities, ethnic groups, and backgrounds. They may have been born into a Muslim family or they may have converted to Islam by saying sincerely, "There is no god but Allah and Muhammad is the Prophet [messenger] of Allah."

Top: Friends hug and greet each other: "Assalamu aleikum!" and "Id Mubarak!" ("Happy festival!")

Above: Muslim cotton pickers in Samarkand, Uzbekistan.

Right: Many Muslims can recite the whole Qur'an, the Islamic scriptures. They read it with respect and devotion, and refer to it as a guide for their life.

About one thousand million people – one fifth of the world's population – are Muslim. These people, from almost every nationality, make up the "ummah", the world-wide Muslim community. There are almost 50 Muslim-majority countries in Asia and Africa. The country with the largest number of Muslims is Indonesia, where there are about 140 million Muslims.

The Prophet Muhammad

The Prophet Muhammad did not start Islam: he started an Islamic community and Muslims believe that he completed the religion. Islam began with humanity and the first Prophet of Islam was Adam. After him came many other Prophets, including Ibrahim (Abraham), Musa (Moses), Dawud (David), and Isa (Jesus). Many Prophets of Islam are prophets in Judaism and Christianity. For Muslims, the Prophet Muhammad is the last Prophet and he is called "the Seal of the Prophets".

1 *What do you think is meant by the phrases in bold print in the quotation below?*

❝ Today, I have **perfected your religion** for you and completed My favour towards you, and have consented to grant you **Islam as the only religion.** ❞
[*Qur'an 5: 3*]

Top: Two Muslim girls in England, on their way to Qur'an classes, with their Arabic workbooks.

Above: Iranian children board the bus for school.

Left: A Muslim mother and baby in Ghana.

The Five Pillars of Islam and the names of Allah

In this unit you will learn about Islam's most important beliefs.

1 *What matters most to you: your family, being a good friend, doing well at school, a hobby . . . ? List all the things that are important to you, which make you what you are, or to which you hang on when life is difficult. Try to group them under headings. Then pick the "top five" – the ones that hold everything together.*

The Five Pillars of Islam

Sometimes Muslims speak about the "Five Pillars of Islam". They are not referring to actual pillars made of stone but to five actions that form the basic structure of Islam. The Five Pillars are a support for Muslims. They make a Muslim life what it is, all over the world and down the ages.

Shahadah

Declaring faith – saying and meaning: "There is no god but Allah and Muhammad is the Prophet of Allah."

Salah

Praying five times a day, on clean ground, in the direction of Makkah.

Sawm

Fasting during daylight hours for a month each year.

Zakah

Paying one-fortieth of annual savings to be given, for example, to people who are poor or suffering.

Hajj

Pilgrimage to Makkah, which all Muslims must do at least once in their life if they can.

Pillars at the Sidi Oqba mosque in Kairouan, Tunisia.

2 *Why do you think the five aspects of Islam are called "Pillars"?*

3 *In a group, choose one of the Five Pillars and find out as much as you can about it from this book. (Refer to the Contents, Index, and Glossary.) Roll and stick a piece of white card to make a cylinder. Draw and cut out pictures, and write and cut out poems and other writings, on the theme of the Pillar you have chosen. Stick them on your cylinder. Share your Pillar with other groups.*

Fingering a tazbi while reciting the names of Allah. The tassel at the end gives a clear starting and finishing point.

The names of Allah

Many Muslims use a "tazbi" when they say their personal prayers. It usually has 99 beads, each representing one of the 99 names of Allah which are given in the Qur'an, the Islamic scriptures. As Muslims finger each bead, they think about a name of Allah and what it means. Fingering the beads helps them to concentrate and keep track. Sometimes the tazbi has only 33 beads and is used three times.

"Where I come from, we say we have a kind of code in our hands. The lines on your right hand are like the Arabic numbers for 81 and the lines on your left hand are like the Arabic numbers for 18. They add up to 99. In the Qur'an there are 99 names for Allah, saying what Allah is like – for example, Kind and Fair. So, in our two hands, we have the names of Allah. "
[*Mustafa, aged 13, who was born in Lebanon*]

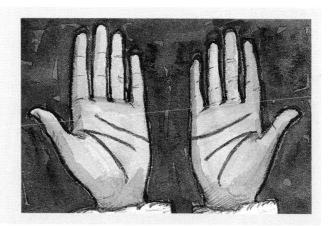

Look at the main lines on the palms of your hands. You have (more or less!) the same lines as in the drawing.

"100 is special in Arabic numbers. It's perfect and complete. We say that Allah has 100 names and there are 99 in the Qur'an. So we know a lot about Allah but we can't know everything because Allah is above us. My uncle says that camels know the 100th name of Allah – but they don't know the 99 – and that's why they have a funny wink! I don't know whether to believe him! "
[*Subaida, aged 12, who was born in Morocco*]

The One and Only God

There is no single, continuous story of creation in the Qur'an. But verses scattered throughout the Qur'an describe how Allah created the earth and everything in it. In English, Muslims use capital letters not only for Allah's name but also for words that refer to Allah.

Allah created everything

Allah is the One and Only God. Allah was never born and will never die. Allah has no parents, no wife, and no children. Allah knows everything and can do anything. Allah made everything for a reason. There is nobody and nothing like Allah.

Allah created the earth and the heavens in six days. They were of one piece. Then He parted them and raised the sky like a roof. He created the night and the day, and the sun and the moon that float in their own orbits, and made the sun, moon, and stars obey His commands.

He spread the earth and laid down firm hills that would not quake or shift, and rivers that would help people find their way. He made the winds blow and sent rain to make the plants grow and for people to drink. Allah provided everything that people need. All that Allah created was good.

Tile work on a mosque in Isfahan. The design gives a feeling of nature and creation. It also contains calligraphy of some verses from the Qur'an.

The creation of people

Allah told the angels, "I'm going to put someone in charge of the world, as my representative on earth." They protested, "Why must you put someone there who'll do harm and cause violence when we sing your praises all the time?" Allah replied, "Don't you think I know what you don't know!" And they said, "It's true that we only know whatever You tell us because You are All Knowing and Wise." So Allah shaped a person from clay and called him Adam. He breathed His spirit into him, and gave him sight and hearing, knowledge, and understanding.

Allah told the angels to bow down to Adam and they did. Iblis was proud and jealous of Adam, and refused. "You created Adam from clay but you created me from fire," he said. "I'm better than him!" Allah cursed Iblis and said, "Get out!" Iblis became Adam's enemy – and the enemy of everyone descended from Adam.

Allah taught Adam the names of plants and animals and asked the angels if they could say the names, but they could not. "We only know what You have taught us," they explained, "for you are All Knowing and Wise." Then Allah asked Adam to say the names and he did.

The creation of woman

Allah asked Adam to live in Paradise and created Eve as a partner for Adam. From them come all the men and women in the world. Allah said to Adam, "Live with your wife in this beautiful garden. You can both eat any fruit, but this one tree is wrong for you. Don't go near it! And watch out for Iblis who's trying to destroy you!"

But Adam and Eve let Iblis tempt them to the tree. Allah said, "You'll fall from Paradise now and live on earth all your life." Adam and Eve were really sorry for what they did but Allah, who is All Merciful, forgave them. "I will give you and all people guidance for your life. If you follow it, you will be happy and, when you die, you'll return to Paradise."

The Alhambra Gardens in Granada were created when Spain was an Islamic country. The gardens are still, for many people, an image of Paradise.

 Draw a picture or create a collage to illustrate "All that Allah created was good." Do not try to draw or show Allah.

Islamic art and creation

Muslims never make pictures or statues of Allah because He has no body. Islamic artists show praise of Allah through geometric patterns which reflect the intricate design of creation; through flowery, leafy patterns suggesting the beauty of Paradise; and through calligraphy of Qur'anic verses.

 Debate whether humans have free will (i.e. can choose to do good or bad, no matter what they have been taught, how they have been brought up, or whether they are happy or not). Divide into two groups to prepare and then present your case, with one group saying that people do have free will and the other group saying that people don't have free will.

Four Men and One Woman

The story in this unit is a re-telling of a folk tale from Saudi Arabia. There are no woods or lions in Saudi Arabia so the story may have come originally from another country. The story conveys some Islamic ideas about creation and creativity.

A carpenter, a tailor, a jeweller, and a student of the Qur'an were travelling together and spent the night in a wood. As there were lions there, they agreed to take turns at keeping watch.

The carpenter's turn came first. He was afraid that he would become drowsy or get bored and fall asleep. So, by the light of the moon, he found a piece of wood and began chipping away until he'd carved a statue of a woman. Then he shook the tailor and said to him, "It's your turn now to keep guard!"

The tailor thought the statue needed some clothes. He made garments from leaves and grass, and dressed the statue in a complete outfit. Then he woke the jeweller, so that he could take over the watch.

The statue seemed rather plain to the jeweller, and so he made earrings, a necklace, and a bracelet of small stones. Pleased with this jewellery, he woke the student for his turn at watching.

The statue looked very beautiful to the student and yet he felt sad. "There's nothing left to make," he thought, "and anyway I don't have any skills like the carpenter, the tailor, and the jeweller."

Just before dawn, he washed, unrolled his prayer mat, and offered morning prayers. He added a prayer of his own: "Lord of the world, I cannot carve wood, sew clothes, or make jewellery. But I beg You to turn this statue into a real woman." Suddenly, the statue began to move and talk. It had become a living woman!

When morning came, the other three woke up and realised that the dead wood had become a woman; the leaves and grass had become a velvet robe; and the stones had become precious jewels. Each person said that the woman was his and they began to argue.

"I started her!" exclaimed the carpenter. "If it hadn't been for me, there wouldn't have been a statue at all!"

"But you left her naked!" accused the tailor. "I was the one who clothed her."

"And you left her looking very plain, tailor!" shouted the jeweller. "I decorated her with jewels which made her beautiful. And as for you, carpenter, you may have started her but I completed her!"

They went on and on squabbling, getting angrier and ruder all the time and almost becoming violent. In the end, they decided to take the matter to court and let the judge decide. The judge listened intently to what had happened and thought carefully about what it meant. Finally, he pronounced his verdict.

"Carpenter, you carved the statue from a piece of dead wood. You, tailor, clothed it with leaves and grass. And you adorned it with stones, jeweller. These are important. But it is the spirit that gives life. The woman would never be alive if the student of the Qur'an hadn't prayed to Allah, the Creator, to breathe life into her. The woman is therefore his and you three can have no share in her."

1 *Do you agree with the judge's verdict? What else could the judge have decided? Think of as many ideas as you can and rank them in order of fairness. If the woman could speak, who might she say she belonged to?*

2 *The events in the story didn't actually happen. The story is a parable about creation and creativity. What do you think is the meaning of the story? How does this story compare with the creation story from the Qur'an that appears in Unit Three?*

3 *The story also has a moral message. Try to sum up what the message is. Create a slogan that the woman/statue could wear on a badge.*

4 *What do you think are the differences between a robot, a human being, and an (other) animal? What, for you, is human about a human being?*

11

FIVE

The Prophet Muhammad's early life and revelation

In this unit you will learn about the Prophet Muhammad's early life in Makkah; and about his experience of revelation in 610 CE.

Life in Makkah

The Prophet Muhammad was born in 570 CE, in the Arabian city of Makkah. The Makkan people were idol worshippers, and many of them traded in idols.

The Prophet Muhammad's father died before the child was born and his mother died when he was six. He was brought up by a foster mother, his grandfather, and then by an uncle.

His uncle was poor and the Prophet Muhammad had to go out to work. The two men went on business trips together. The Prophet Muhammad could not read or write. However, because of his honesty and wisdom, he was called "the trustworthy". When he was 25, his uncle arranged for him to look after and deliver some merchandise belonging to Khadijah, a wealthy widow aged 40. Khadijah was so impressed with the Prophet Muhammad's work that she proposed to him. He accepted and they were married.

Revelation

As a young man, the Prophet Muhammad spent hours in the cave of Hira, near Makkah, thinking about life and what things mean, what good and bad are, why we are born . . . On the 27th of the month of Ramadan in 610 CE, he was frightened to hear a strong voice. He asked who or what it was and heard "Recite!" He felt himself being grabbed and hugged firmly – and then being let go. After this had happened three times, he asked, "What shall I recite?" The voice said, "Recite! In the name of your Lord . . ." The Prophet Muhammad knew that the voice was that of the Angel Jibril (Gabriel) and that the message spoken through him was from Allah.

Each year on one of the last ten nights of the month of Ramadan, the Prophet Muhammad received another part of the message – 23 times altogether. First he told his wife, Khadijah, and she accepted what he said. Then he told his friends and relatives, and other members of his tribe. They accepted what he said, but most people in Makkah did not. Perhaps this was because the main part of the message was that

Visitors to the Cave of the Prophet, today.

there is only one God – and the Makkans believed in and traded in idols. They reacted violently to the message.

The Qur'an is made up of all the revelations from Allah to the Prophet Muhammad.

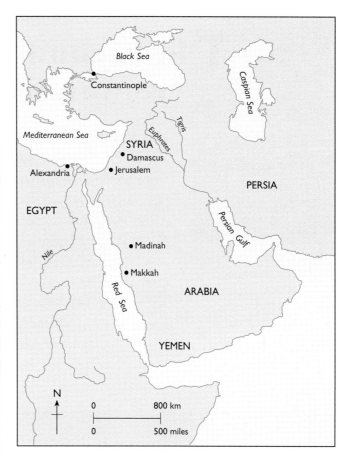

The Pledge

A trader from Yemen had been cheated by some Makkan traders and asked for help – but no one responded. So he wrote and recited a sarcastic poem about the people of Makkah. One of the Prophet Muhammad's uncles heard the poem and it made him feel bad. He called a meeting of the elders of Makkah and set up an organisation which pledged to help anyone who was being oppressed – local people or foreigners. The Prophet Muhammad was quite young but became a keen member of the organisation. He said, "I will not give up being a member even for a herd of camels. If anyone appeals to me, because of that pledge, I will hurry to help them."

The Black Stone

The Ka'aba ("cube") is in the centre of Makkah. Muslims believe that it was built by Ibrahim (Abraham) and his son Ismail (Ishmael) when Allah commanded Ibrahim to sacrifice Ismail. Beneath the Ka'aba is the altar built by Adam for the worship of Allah.

The Ka'aba has a special black stone in one corner. Once the Ka'aba burned to the ground and all the tribes of Makkah helped build it again. But they quarrelled because they all wanted the honour of putting back the black stone. They decided that the Prophet Muhammad should judge who should do it – and he did! He laid a white sheet on the ground, placed the black stone on it, and asked the people to hold the sheet round the edge. Then together they carried the stone to the Ka'aba and the Prophet fixed the stone in its place.

1 *What kind of things do you wonder about when you are alone and quiet?*

2 *If someone told you of new ideas and said that they came from a voice he or she had heard, what would make you believe or disbelieve it? How would that person believe himself or herself?*

3 *What do the stories of "The Pledge" and "The Black Stone" say about the Prophet Muhammad?*

4 *Using information from this and the following unit, draw a time-line of events in the Prophet Muhammad's life. Use dates (not ages of the Prophet). Create small sketches to represent each event. But do not portray the Prophet or any of his followers. Muslims believe that this would make them into idols.*

The beginning of the Islamic community

The Night Journey

For thirteen years, the Prophet Muhammad and his followers in Makkah were persecuted for the new ideas they preached. Muslims believe that, in 621, during the saddest and most difficult time for the Prophet in Makkah, Allah gave him a special privilege – a vision of meeting Allah. Muslims call this the "Night Journey".

The Prophet himself described how the Angel Jibril (Gabriel) woke him and took him from Makkah to Jerusalem on an animal like a horse with wings. In Jerusalem, he met all the earlier Prophets. Then he climbed the seven heavens of creation. Beyond the seventh heaven he passed through the veils that cover what is hidden, until he reached the veil of Unity and looked at what eyes cannot see and minds cannot imagine. All this happened in just a moment.

The first Islamic community

In 622, when the Prophet's life was threatened and the followers of Islam were in danger, they fled Makkah for a town that was later called Madinah. This is called the "hijra" (migration). The first Islamic community was started in Madinah, and the year 622 is the beginning of the Islamic calendar.

In 624, a large army from Makkah marched on Madinah. Many of the soldiers were killed or

The "Dome of the Rock" in Jerusalem was built over the rock from which the Prophet ascended.

The rock itself, inside the beautiful domed building.

Makkah and Madinah, in a Turkish manuscript.

captured by the Prophet's supporters, and the rest fled back to Makkah. After two more battles the Prophet eventually persuaded the Makkans to sign a peace treaty.

The Prophet spent the next few years preaching Islam outside Madinah. He sent Muslims to the rulers of neighbouring lands, to invite them to accept Islam. In 630, after the Makkans had broken the peace treaty many times, the Prophet said that they had either to respect the treaty or deny it. The Makkans denied the treaty and the Prophet and his followers captured Makkah. Since then, Makkah has been the "capital" of the Islamic world.

In 631, the Prophet gave his "Farewell Sermon" in the Valley of Arafat and a year later he died. His death sent shock-waves through the Muslim community. They decided to recognise Abu Bakr, the Prophet's father-in-law, as his Caliph – successor – but only as a leader, not as a prophet. When Abu Bakr died two years later, he was succeeded by Umar. Umar called himself "Commander of the Faithful" and this became the title of the Caliphs. After Umar came Utman and Ali, who moved the centre of the community from Madinah to Iraq. These four Caliphs, who ruled from 632 to 661, are the most important and are known as "rightly guided Caliphs". At that time, there was dispute as to whether Caliphs should be actual descendants or simply chosen for their good qualities.

The Prophet's Mosque in Madinah, today. It is expanded from the first mosque in the world, on a spot which the Prophet Muhammad chose.

Part of the Prophet's last sermon
❝ One day you will **appear before Allah** and **answer for your deeds**. So beware! Do not stray from the **path of righteousness** after I am gone . . . No prophet or apostle will come after me and no new faith will be born . . . Reflect on my words. I leave behind two things, the Qur'an and **my example**, and if you **follow these guides** you will not fail . . . All those who listen to me shall pass on my words to others, and those to others again; and may the last ones understand my words better than those who listen to me directly . . . ❞

1 *Discuss the meaning of the phrases in bold print in the quotation above.*

2 *Do you think that you will have to answer for your good and bad deeds when you die?*

SEVEN

What It's Worth (part one)

This unit and the next tell a story about Utman, the third Caliph. The story is set in Madinah about 1400 years ago.

1 *Allot parts in the story, and read it out as a radio play. Devout Muslims do not portray Prophets and Caliphs in pictures or through a visible actor; but actors can portray Prophets and Caliphs just through their voices.*

Characters

Narrator
Utman, the third Caliph
Laila, a young girl
Laila's brother
Laila's parents
A muezzin (someone who calls people to prayer)
First trader, one of the richest in Madinah

Second trader, a buyer and seller of camels
Third and fourth traders, two sisters who deal in spices
Fifth trader, a metal smith
Sixth trader, a dried-fruit merchant
Seventh trader, a silk dealer
Eighth trader, a jeweller

First trader:	The sun has hardly risen and already it's stronger than I can bear.
Narrator:	For months there has been no rain and the land is dry. The water cisterns are empty and people's throats are parched.
Second trader:	If nothing happens soon, even our hope will dry out.
Narrator:	The crops have long since been eaten and nothing will grow in the cracked soil of Madinah, the city so loved by the Prophet Muhammad – the first home of the Islamic community.
Third and fourth traders:	It's hard to imagine that, before the famine, Madinah was an oasis in the desert, a fresh and vibrant spot of scorching sand as far as the eye could see. Who'd have thought that all our shops would be shut now, our stalls folded away, and the travelling merchants long gone?
Fifth trader:	I remember not so long ago when Madinah was bustling and noisy. Now it's so deserted, it's eerie. And the only sounds you can hear are the call to prayer five times a day and the pitiful cries of starving babies.
Narrator:	For a while, rich families had still had water from their private wells and food from the stocks that they had laid in, but now these too have run out. Lounging under the shade of palm trees, people can only dream of sipping cool drinks, sucking slices of juicy melon, and chewing dates.
	From beneath a canopy on the flat roof of her home, Laila suddenly leaps up in excitement, pointing a finger across the desert.
Laila:	Look! There's something shimmering on the horizon.
Laila's brother:	It's a mirage, stupid!

Narrator:	Laila's family all look, but see nothing. Laila's right, though. Making its way over the sand dunes is the heavily laden camel caravan of Utman, the third Caliph, a rich, respected businessman who's been on a shopping trip.
Laila's parents:	We're saved!
Narrator:	By the time the caravan nears the gates of the city, the whole neighbourhood has heard about what Laila has seen. Some people even run out through the city gates and over the burning hot sand to meet Utman, tugging at his caftan and almost pulling him off his camel.
Fifth trader:	What did you get?
First trader:	I'll take the lot!
Utman:	[with a wave of the hand] No. Sorry!
Second trader:	I'll double the offer!
Utman:	No chance!
Third and fourth traders:	We'll pay you three times what it cost you.
Utman:	No way!
Fifth trader:	I can raise that to four!
Utman:	Nothing doing, I'm afraid!
Sixth trader:	Five!
Utman:	Not interested!
Seventh trader:	I'll go up to six times what the load is worth! How would you like it? Cloth? Perfume? Gems? Gold?
Utman:	Madam, I don't care how you pay, because you're not paying!
Eighth trader:	Now here's an offer you can't refuse! Seven – S-E-V-E-N – times what you paid, cash in hand!

2 *Why do you think that Utman was not selling the goods he had brought to Madinah? If you had had goods to sell, would you have sold them to the traders? Why?*

3 *What do you imagine is going to happen next in the story?*

EIGHT

What It's Worth (part two)

In this unit you will discover the ending of the story of Utman which began in Unit Seven.

Narrator: With crowds pressing all around, Utman reaches the gateway into Madinah and gets down from his camel.

Utman: Look, you can make me offers until the camels come home, but this food is NOT for sale – simply because it belongs to someone else who is paying me ten times what it's worth.

All traders: *[gasping in disbelief]* Ten times?

Utman: That's right! Now would you please let me pass?

Narrator: There was a stunned silence.

Seventh trader: Whoever could that be?

Eighth trader: There's only one way to find out – that's to follow Utman!

Narrator: The traders catch up with Utman and tag along behind as he heads for downtown Madinah. Here he unloads his camel bags on to the streets and hands out armfuls of food to the poor people of the city.

Utman: *[speaking to the poor people]* Allah is great! Come to eat!

Narrator: Utman's actions are beyond the poor people's wildest dreams and Utman sees their sad expressions change into looks of surprise, smiles of thankfulness, and tears of joy.

All traders: [*angrily*] Liar! Cheat! No one has paid you ten times what the goods were worth! You deserve to be . . . !

Utman: Allah is the someone! Look at the difference it's made to these wonderful people. Don't you remember what it says in our Holy Qur'an? . . . that if you do something good, Allah will reward you ten times over.

Narrator: In the distance, the muezzin is calling from the minar of the mosque, at the set time.

Muezzin: [*calling loudly*] Come to prayer! Come to success!

1 Are you surprised at the outcome of the story?

2 In what way would Utman get paid by Allah ten times over?

A muezzin calls Muslims to prayer from the minar of the Kashgar mosque in China.

The Prophet's Mosque in Madinah, at dusk.

3 Do people usually get rewarded for the good things they do? In what way? Do people usually get punished for the bad things they do? In what way?

4 What does this story tell us about Islamic beliefs and values?

Getting ready for prayer

This is the first of two units about prayer. Here you will find out about the importance of prayer for Muslims, and how Muslims get ready for prayer.

1 *It says in the Qur'an (20:14): "Establish salah [prayer] to remember me." Who do you think "me" is?*

2 *A saying of the Prophet Muhammad is: "Say part of your prayers at home so that your houses do not become like graves." What do you think "like graves" might mean?*

"Salah", praying five times a day, is one of the Five Pillars of Islam (see page 6). The Qur'an speaks of salah and the Prophet Muhammad was known to offer salah.

The place for prayer

When they can, Muslims pray together, but they may pray on their own. Muslims perform salah wherever they are, provided the place is clean. It could be at home, at school or work, or on a journey. When Muslims are away from home and their local community, they carry a "sajjadah" (prayer mat). They use it to pray anywhere where the ground may not be clean.

To keep their home clean – especially the place where they pray – many families leave their outdoor shoes at the front door.

Men at different stages of wudhu outside the Old Delhi Jamia Mosque in India.

3 *If you overheard people teasing Nasima or other Muslims about praying, what would you say: to them? to her? Think about what you already know about Islam to answer this.*

❝ Some of my friends at school think it must be a drag to have to pray. It *is* something we have to do, but I don't see it like that. I really like it. You get a bit of time out – just a few minutes each time – for some peace of mind, and I feel that I can speak to Allah. I love the feeling that Muslims everywhere are praying five times a day and have been for over 1400 years. It gives our lives a sort of shape. But some kids who don't like us tease us about praying. If they see that we're finding the lesson hard or we're upset about something, they say sarcastic things like, 'Are you going to say your prayers now, then?' ❞
[Nasima Begum, a teenage Muslim girl of a Bangladeshi family]

Wudhu

Before salah, Muslims wash in a special way called "wudhu". They wash their hands, mouth, nose, face, arms, head, ears, neck, and feet three times in running water. If there's no water for wudhu, for example in the desert, Muslims place both hands lightly on earth, sand, stone, or something with dust on it; then blow the dust off their hands and wipe their face once with their hands. Then they touch the dust again, and wipe each arm up to the elbow.

Facing towards the Ka'aba

All over the world, Muslims turn to the Ka'aba, in Makkah, for salah. A "Makkah compass" is a magnetic compass with numbers around the edge and a solid bar "pointing" to the Ka'aba. To use it, you have to know the number for the place where you are (Britain is 25). You turn the compass so that the needle points to that number. Then the solid bar shows you the direction of the Ka'aba. This is roughly south-east in Britain. Some sajjadahs have a Makkah compass on them.

This "spacetronic" watch has a built-in Makkah compass.

> **4** *Create a poster about the wudhu sequence that might be displayed near the washing and prayer areas in a mosque or in an Islamic school.*

A man, on a journey, prays alone by the river Indus.

The wudhu sequence
- say, "In the name of Allah, the Most Merciful, the Most Kind"
- wash both hands three times up to the wrist
- rinse mouth three times
- sniff water into nostrils three times
- wash tip of nose three times
- wash face three times
- wash right arm, from wrist to elbow, then left arm
- move palm of hand over hair, from forehead to back of head
- pass both hands over head to neck
- rub fingers in grooves and holes of ears and pass thumbs behind ears
- wash right foot thoroughly up to ankles, then left foot

Praying with hundreds of others – too many to fit into the mosque – in Alexandria, Egypt.

TEN

Time for prayer

In this second unit about prayer you will learn about the times of prayer for Muslims and the sequence of prayer movements ("rak'ahs").

The prayer times

Muslims pray five times each day: once during each of five set periods. The times are set by the place of the sun in the sky, and vary from one season to another. Timetables are printed showing when each prayer period begins and ends. Also, most mosques have clock boards showing the times for prayer.

In Islamic societies, the call to prayer (the "adhan") is heard five times a day. It is given by the muezzin from the minar or the courtyard of the mosque. It is also broadcast on the radio.

A clock board showing times of daily and of Friday noon prayers.

THE FIVE TIMES OF DAILY PRAYERS		
Arabic name	English name	Period during which prayers are said
Fajr	Dawn	From early dawn until just before sunrise
Zuhr	Noon	From just after noon until mid-afternoon
Asr	Afternoon	From mid-afternoon until just before sunset
Maghrib	Evening	From sunset until the light of day has gone
Isha	Night	During the hours of darkness until just before dawn

1 Make a day's timetable for one of the following Muslims in Britain today. The timetable should show all the things the person does in a day, including performing salah. You will need to find out when sunrise, noon, and sunset are – from today's newspaper, for example. Mark on the timetable the prayer times that the person might find it hard to keep exactly.
▶ a secondary school pupil
▶ someone who stays at home and looks after children
▶ a night shift worker
▶ someone who works in an office or shop

Praying at home, using sajjadahs on top of the carpet. Makkah and Madinah are represented on the sajjadahs, within the decorative borders.

Prayer movements

When a Muslim prays, it is with the whole body, not just the head or the heart. The words used and the "rak'ahs" (prayer movements) come from the ways that the Prophet Muhammad prayed.

A rak'ah literally means "bending", and each movement has a special meaning. If they can't make the rak'ahs, for example if they have broken their leg or if they are on an aeroplane, Muslims "perform" them in their heart.

Salah begins with Muslims saying that they are going to pray, as this helps them to concentrate on prayer and to pray sincerely. All Muslims offer salah in Arabic. Some Muslims also offer personal prayers of their own.

Muslims recite "Al-Fatihah" at least seventeen times a day, during the five times of salah. It comes at the beginning of the Qur'an and you can read it on page 39.

2 Imagine you are creating a book for a Muslim child about salah. Prepare a section of the book about rak'ahs, using drawings and captions.

Using a handkerchief as a "mini" sajjadah.

The sequence of a rak'ah

1. stand straight, saying how many rak'ahs (2, 3, or 4) there will be
2. bring hands up to ears (for males) or to shoulders (for females) and say, "Allah is the Greatest"
3. place right hand on left hand, on chest (for females) or just below the navel (for males), say, "Allah, glory and praise are for You", and then recite the opening sura of the Qur'an (see page 39)
4. bow down, with hands on knees, saying three times, "Glory to my God, the Great"
5. stand, saying, "Allah hears those who praise Him . . ."
6. kneel and stretch right out, with knees, forehead, and palms touching the floor (females with hands at chest level, males with hands stretched out in front), saying, "Glory to my God, in the Highest"
7. sit straight, on left foot, with palms on knees and right foot slightly to right of leg and heel straight up, saying, "Allah is most Great"
8. as in 6, saying "Allah is Most Great" and then, three times, "Glory to my God, Allah"
9. stand, saying, "Allah is Most Great (this is the end of one rak'ah)
10. repeat the sequence 1, 2, or 3 times, then finally turn face to right and say, "Peace and the Mercy of Allah be on you", and turn face to left and say the same

Praying outside, this man uses a sajjadah which he carries with him.

ELEVEN

Zakah

This unit is about the importance of giving in Islam.

> **1** *"What's mine is mine!"*
> *"What's mine is yours!"*
> *"What's mine is God's!"*
> *These are three different points of view about things we have. Discuss with a partner what you think each of them means, and say which one you most agree with and why.*

A couple count their savings to calculate the zakah they need to pay.

Zakah is one of the Five Pillars of Islam (see page 6) and it has two meanings. The main meaning is "giving to charity".

Muslims believe that they should try to help others and should give money to help people who are suffering or in need. Muslims give 2.5 per cent of their savings as zakah each year. This means that they give 2.5 per cent of what they have left, in cash, in the bank, in gold and silver, after they have paid all their own bills.

In some Islamic societies, the government collects zakah as a kind of tax. In other parts of the world, paying zakah is left up to each Muslim – but they are all supposed to pay it. Muslims pay zakah on the festival of Id-ul-Fitr (see pages 27 and 29).

Zakah ensures that wealth is shared within the Muslim community.

The second meaning of "zakah" is "purity". Sajidah Ulami, a Muslim businesswoman, explains: "In Islam, there's nothing wrong with making money and having money. But we have to understand that we have a duty to use our money for other Muslims as well as for ourselves. When we pay zakah, it purifies what we have. We say that everything comes from Allah and returns to Allah."

What zakah can be spent on:
- helping the poor and the needy
- paying the wages of zakah collectors
- freeing hostages and debtors
- people on a journey who are in need
- the daily needs of students of the Qur'an
- for "winning over hearts" to Islam
- for any action in the cause of Allah

> **2** *Why is a time of celebration (such as the festival of Id-ul-Fitr) an especially good occasion to give money to charity?*

> **3** *What are the good points about everyone paying the same percentage of their savings rather than everyone paying the same amount? What are the good points about zakah being a percentage of people's savings rather than a percentage of their income?*

Sadakah

As well as the annual zakah, some Muslims give money to charity at other times. This is called sadakah, and some families and communities have collection boxes for it.

> " Once my uncle wanted to pay my dad for something but my dad didn't want to take the money. He said it was a gift but my uncle thought it was too much to take without paying. So he popped the money in the sadakah box and that settled it! "
> [Shafiq, aged 12]

Welfare agencies

Today there are several national and international Islamic welfare agencies. The best-known are Islamic Aid and Muslim Relief. These organisations depend on zakah and sadakah from Muslims all over the world.

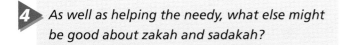

4 As well as helping the needy, what else might be good about zakah and sadakah?

5 Create a poster that could be displayed at a mosque or in an Islamic school, about a Muslim welfare organisation to which zakah money might be given.

Yusuf Islam, a well-known British Muslim, pumps water by hand on a visit to West Sudan Green Camp, an Islamic aid project.

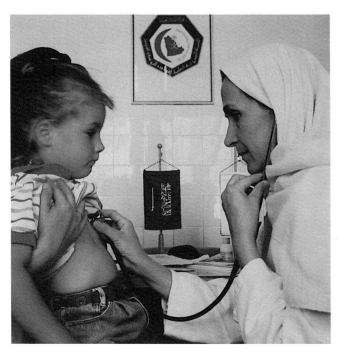

Advertising a children's charity in Mashhad, Iran.

A Muslim doctor examines a child at a clinic supported by money from Saudi Arabia, in Sarajevo, Bosnia.

TWELVE

Fasting in Ramadan

1 What do "fasting", "starving", and "dieting" mean? What is similar about them and what is different?

2 Have you ever said, "I'm starving!"? What did you mean?

3 Find out all you can about the health benefits of fasting in moderation.

Fasting can be good for the body. Also, by fasting, people gain an understanding of what it is like to be very hungry and so may come to feel greater compassion for those who are truly starving. However, the main reason that Muslims fast is that it teaches them self-discipline – they realise that they can take control of their body and that there is more to life than feeling full.

66 O you who believe! Fasting is prescribed to you as it was prescribed to those before you that you may learn self-restraint. 99
[Qur'an 2: 183]

Ramadan

Unless it is bad for their health, all adult Muslims have to fast during the hours of daylight every day in the month of Ramadan, the ninth month of the Islamic year. Fasting, or "sawm", at this time is one of the Five Pillars of Islam (see page 6). The month is also a time for spiritual refreshment, when Muslims try extra hard to be patient and kind.

Ramadan is the most important month of the Islamic year because it was in that month, for 23 years, that the Prophet Muhammad received Allah's message. Read about this on page 12.

Pupils at an Islamic school in Britain study the moon as part of their work in science.

In Islam, a month begins with a new moon and lasts 29 or 30 days. There are twelve months in the Islamic year, making 354 days. This means that, on the international calendar used in everyday life, Ramadan comes about eleven days earlier each year than the year before. It takes about 30 years for Ramadan to "come round" again to the same time on the international calendar.

Some Muslims have special calendars and diaries where Ramadan is shown on tinted paper, often green. This is a practical help and it serves to remind Muslims of Ramadan all year long.

 4 *In what way is a calendar or diary showing Ramadan a practical help?*

The beginning and end of the fast

Muslims wait for the new moon to be sighted at the beginning of Ramadan, before they begin the fast. Muslim leaders take responsibility for announcing the new moon and in Islamic societies the announcement is broadcast on radio and television.

In some places, a siren or other loud noise signals the end of each day's fast and this is also announced on the radio.

When the next new moon is sighted, Ramadan is over. The Id-ul-Fitr festival follows.

Fireworks and fun in the Hari Raya celebrations at the end of Ramadan in Sumatra, Indonesia.

 5 *Write out the passage below, filling in the blanks with a word or phrase. You will need to refer to pages 12-13, 14-15, and 28-29 for some information.*

Ramadan is the ninth month in the _____ calendar. It lasts _____ or _____ days. Ramadan is the month when the _____ was revealed to _____ by Allah, through _____ .

During Ramadan, most Muslims fast between _____ and _____. Fasting means not _____, not _____, not smoking, and not having sexual contact. There are several reasons given for fasting: one of them is that _____. Some Muslims do not have to fast, for example _____. Some Muslims should not fast, for example _____.

Throughout Ramadan, Muslims try especially hard to _____. On the first day of the following month, there is a festival called _____.

THIRTEEN

Two views of Ramadan

In this unit you can read about Ramadan from two different people's points of view.

A Muslim family in England

Khadijah Miah works in a school canteen. She and her husband were brought up in Pakistan. Their children were born in England. Below is Khadijah's description of Ramadan.

An evening meal in Ramadan. It is a custom to break the fast with dates, as the Prophet Muhammad did.

❝ Only two of us canteen workers are Muslims. The other one was pregnant last Ramadan so she couldn't fast, but usually she does.

During Ramadan, if we need to check something like salt, one of the other cooks tastes it. While the others have elevenses, we just sit outside or carry on working.

Normally, when we've served the meals and cleared up, we all have our dinner before going home. In Ramadan I go home as soon as I have cleared up. I try to have a lie-down before my children get home. The mornings are OK when we are fasting. The afternoons are harder.

A Ramadan day is quite different from any other. We start fasting before dawn and finish after sunset. When Ramadan falls in summer, we get up and eat very early, before it's light, then go back to bed until it's time to go to school or work. Your habits change, too – for instance, you don't come in and put the kettle on straight away!

One of my daughters is at secondary school and she's already fasting. Usually she helps me cook supper but in Ramadan she can't stand smelling the food before she is allowed to eat it! I don't think her school is very good about Ramadan because there's nowhere for the Muslim children to go at dinner time.

My husband works in a factory. In Ramadan, when he's on the night shift, he can eat during breaks, but when he's on days it's not so good. There's only the cafeteria and the rest room for people to go to. My husband was brought up as a Muslim in Pakistan, like me, and so Ramadan matters a lot to him. It's an important part of our religion to have discipline and go without things. ❞

 What are the links between famine and Ramadan?

 What could the managers of the factory do in Ramadan to make conditions better?

At school

Peter Jones, a head of year in a secondary school, says:

Soft drinks, balloons, and all the fun of the fair on Id-ul-Fitr outside a British mosque.

" I'm not a Muslim, but I try to understand Islam as it's an important religion and we have Muslims in our school and our society. I went to Tunisia for a holiday during Ramadan, so I've seen it first hand.

I look after all the pupils in my year and I think everyone should be able to keep their religion. It's hard for Muslim pupils in Ramadan, when everyone else is eating, and so I try to make sure that teachers and tutors know what it means and what's going on. Some understand well, but some think that everyone should be treated the same.

We've introduced 'Ramadan rooms' – one for girls and one for boys. Muslims can go there, away from food, and just sit quietly or pray. Sometimes Muslims don't feel up to doing PE in Ramadan. That can create difficulties with the PE staff.

This year the Humanities teachers have been doing work on famine and they say there are good links with Ramadan.

We often have to deal with pupils who don't see Ramadan in a very positive way. They don't understand or just can't cope with people who are different. We had an unfortunate incident with a girl who doesn't swallow her saliva when she's fasting. So she carries a little plastic container with her and privately spits into it. Someone saw it and she got called all sorts of names. The whole thing was horrible.

When it comes to Id-ul-Fitr, the day after Ramadan ends, most Muslim pupils and staff are off school as it's a festival. But, after that, we have a special assembly and put up signs and decorations. "

3 *What might Peter Jones say or do to non-Muslim pupils in his school who have spoken or acted unkindly towards Muslim pupils? What might the pupils say to him?*

4 *Create a page for the School Staff Bulletin, giving the information that you think staff ought to have about Ramadan.*

5 *Create a dialogue between two teachers or tutors at the school who have different ideas about arrangements for Muslim pupils.*

FOURTEEN

Preparing for Hajj

Ever since Soofia was little, she'd wanted to go on Hajj to Makkah. It seemed so exciting and holy, something to bring her closer to other Muslims and to Allah. It would change her life, she thought . . . It was never just that she *had* to go: she really *wanted* to.

She expected that her husband Karim would want to wait until they'd settled into their home. He'll probably say there's no rush, she thought, and that we've got our whole lives ahead of us . . . Soofia knew that she couldn't go to Makkah alone or with another woman – but only with her husband, father, or brother. Her brothers were still at school and her father was not well. So, if she was going at all, it would be with Karim. Anyway, it seemed right to go with her husband.

Karim thought it was a great idea! But he wondered if they could get the time off work and if they could afford the fares and accommodation. They would have to make sure that they could leave without owing anything and still have a little money to come back to. They would need to work hard and save all they could. Karim agreed that it was better to go on Hajj before they had children. "It'll be lovely to tell the children about our Hajj," Soofia added. "I want them to know we went to Makkah in our early married life. They'll see that being Muslim is important to us: it'll help strengthen their faith."

Practical arrangements

Luckily, a crowd from the mosque was going on Hajj that year. They could make arrangements together. They had to apply to the Saudi Arabian Embassy for Hajj visas for entry into Saudi Arabia and into Makkah itself. Only Muslims can go to Makkah. It helped to get the visas through the mosque. Next Soofia and Karim booked their flight. The airline ran a special Hajj package tour.

Sites visited during the Hajj.

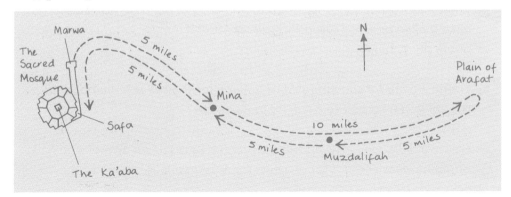

One last thing for Soofia and Karim to do for themselves was to buy some special clothing. Soofia needed a "burka" – a full-length cotton dress with enough material to cover her head. Karim needed an "ihram" – two lengths of white cloth, one to wrap tightly round his waist and the other to drape over his chest and shoulders. Soofia and Karim packed their burka and ihram carefully with their other clothes. They would wear them when they got to Makkah, to feel at one with other Muslims dressed the same way.

Saying goodbye

Friends dropped in to wish Soofia and Karim a safe journey and a wonderful experience. "Think of me when you drink Zamzam water!" one of Soofia's old school friends said jokingly. "And don't think of me when you stone the devil!" added a colleague of Karim.

A team of workers use gold thread to embroider the "kiswa", the black velvet cloth which covers the Ka'aba.

The couple spent the last night with their families. Karim's brother and sister-in-law had been on Hajj and still remembered what someone had said to them in Makkah: "You're travelling to the Ka'aba which is the centre of Islam, and you must also travel to your heart, the centre of your life."

"Pray for your father," Soofia's mother whispered. "He doesn't complain but I know he's not really well."

There were hugs and kisses and tears at the airport. Then Soofia and Karim boarded the plane with their group from the mosque.

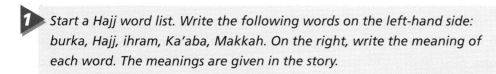

1 ▶ Start a Hajj word list. Write the following words on the left-hand side: burka, Hajj, ihram, Ka'aba, Makkah. On the right, write the meaning of each word. The meanings are given in the story.

2 ▶ With a partner, imagine that one of you is Soofia and the other is Soofia's boss. Make up a dialogue in which Soofia asks for time off work (without pay) to go on Hajj and explains why the journey is so important to her.

3 ▶ Make a list of the things that Muslims have to do to prepare for Hajj.

FIFTEEN

The journey to Makkah

Here is the second part of the story of Soofia and Karim going on Hajj.

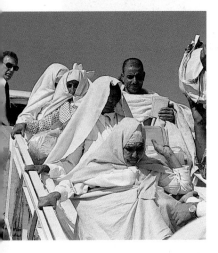

Pilgrims, already in ihram, leave the plane at Jeddah airport.

All the passengers on the plane were on Hajj and many had waited years and spent their life's savings on it. Throughout the flight, someone or other was reciting from the Qur'an and, from time to time, pilgrims would call out to Allah, "Labbaika!" ("Here I am!"). Soofia and Karim felt drawn deeply into the mood of the Hajj.

The plane was to land at Jeddah, the capital of Saudi Arabia. Before landing, Soofia washed in the ritual way that she does before prayers. Then she put on her special clothes, as did Karim and all the other passengers: the plane was transformed! No one could tell now who was rich, poor, famous, or even where anyone came from. They all looked equal to each other's eyes now, just as they always are to Allah. On Hajj, they would make a particular effort to be peaceful – not to fight or even quarrel, and not to harm any living thing.

In Saudi Arabia

After going through customs at Jeddah everyone got a pass to enter Makkah. It was like a local passport, and they had to leave their real passport at Jeddah. The crowded airport was hot and stuffy and Soofia and Karim were relieved when their group's guide and tour leader, Riadh, arrived. His job was to interpret for any Muslims who did not speak Arabic. He had to arrange board and lodging for them and show them how to get around. Riadh seemed friendly and helpful. He said that he would do all he could to make their Hajj a special and spiritual experience.

They set off for Makkah by coach: it was about a two-hour drive across the desert and they had to stop at control posts to show their passes. Soofia hadn't realised how tight the security would be, but obviously the holiness of Makkah had to be preserved and only people who would respect it could be allowed in. Not everyone travelled by coach. Some people went by car, some by donkey or camel. A few even walked. Many of the pilgrims called out again to Allah, "Labbaika!"

When they reached Makkah, Soofia felt her heart skip a beat and she had to pinch herself. Was she finally here? Was this really happening to her? She almost didn't want to enter the city now in case it spoiled the dream she had had for so long. Karim was more practical: they were all hot, tired, and thirsty, and he just wanted to find their hotel!

1 Add "Labbaika" to your Hajj word list, with an explanation of what it means.

2 Begin a Hajj itinerary (list of places visited), starting with Britain.

The Ka'aba

But they couldn't keep away from the Ka'aba for long: it was drawing them like a magnet. So they made for the "sacred house", the central mosque in Makkah. The golden embroidery on the black cloth glinted in the sun and Soofia felt her soul light up! Surely, she thought, the whole world was ablaze with the glory of Allah!

On the road from Jeddah to Makkah. It is a custom to make this trip in the open air and so some pilgrims sit on top of the vehicles.

They joined the swirling crowds and moved around the Ka'aba seven times. Some people had to be carried on stretchers or chairs and Karim saw a very short man held up between the shoulders of his friends. Soofia had never seen so many people. They were pressing in all around her and she let herself be carried along by this river of Muslim faith. She was part of that river now and her heart soared. There was nothing in the world like this: she felt beautiful and free.

A swirling crowd moves round the Ka'aba. Some pilgrims are close enough to the Ka'aba to reach out and touch it.

3 *What kind of things do you think the pilgrims might need to ask their guide to help with?*

4 *Talk with a partner, or write, about a place that has a special meaning for you. What gives it that meaning?*

SIXTEEN

Special events on Hajj

Here is the third part of the story of Soofia and Karim on Hajj.

Zamzam water on sale – to drink there or to take home as a gift or souvenir.

Pilgrims move between Safa and Marwa in two lanes – one going each way – and there is a separate lane in the middle for anyone in a wheel-chair.

Running between Safa and Marwa

It's 366 metres between Safa and Marwa, but Soofia had such energy and joy that she almost sprinted – seven times – between the two hills, pacing out the steps that Hagar had taken, thousands of years ago, in her frantic search for water for her baby boy, Ismail. In desperation, Hagar had returned to where she had left Ismail and, to her delight and amazement, found gushing water. As Soofia drank some Zamzam water, she re-lived some of Hagar's thankfulness: it was the best drink of her life!

The day of Arafat

Next Soofia set off for the tiny town of Mina. The short journey took ages because the thousands of people on the road were moving at a snail's pace, whether in vehicles or on foot. Soofia didn't like this part: it was like a rush-hour traffic jam!

They spent the night in Mina and made an early start for the Plain of Arafat, where over a million pilgrims gathered for prayers at noon. For months, Riadh and the other guides had been getting things ready for the pilgrims' arrival. There were rows of tents, as far as the eye could see. An office in the Saudi Arabian government prepares for Hajj all year round. As soon as one Hajj is over, it organises the clearing up and gets ready for the next year.

Soofia was grateful for the shade inside the tent. She closed her eyes and thought, "If I didn't know there were so many people here, I would think I was completely alone. It's silent for miles around. It seems as if the whole universe is silent now. We're all here, before Allah, with our private thoughts, secret hopes, and deepest prayers. We're alone and together. No wonder the Prophet Muhammad, peace be upon him, said, 'The best of prayers is the prayer on the day of Arafat'."

Food was cooked and served to all the people at Arafat. Each group was given food of the kind eaten in their own country. "What a good idea!" Soofia thought. "Not everyone has the same tastes." She also wondered about Karim. Husbands and wives do not sleep together on Hajj, so Soofia had stayed with other women and Karim with other men. They had seen each other but had not spent any time together. "He's such a fussy eater!" she thought, but then caught a glimpse of him tucking in. "I should have realised . . ." she said to herself. "There's a very special feeling here!"

Back to Mina

As it got dark, the pilgrims set off again — in buses or cars or on foot — chanting prayers all the way. Soofia felt as if her life was just beginning. They spent that night in the desert at Muzdallifah. Some people bedded down. Others lit fires and sat talking. Soofia's feet were aching and she tried to sleep, but she just kept turning everything over in her mind.

They got back to Mina the next day, and found its narrow streets and little squares crowded with souvenir stalls. Soofia bought all sorts of things that she wouldn't look at twice elsewhere. There were also stands selling refreshing cold drinks and slices of juicy fruit.

"The biggest camp site ever": the Plain of Arafat covered in tents.

1 ▶ Add the following to your Hajj word list, with explanations of what they mean: Arafat, Safa and Marwa.

2 ▶ Continue writing the Hajj itinerary.

3 ▶ Make a list of all the things that you think the Hajj office in the Saudi Arabian government has to make arrangements for (e.g. hygiene, security . . .)

SEVENTEEN

The end of the Hajj

Here is the last part of the story of Soofia and Karim on Hajj.

Jamrah

The main part of the stay in Mina was "jamrah" and Soofia went with Karim to stone the pillars. She had been told that you have to feel like Ismail: he was tempted by the devil, but stoned him and drove him away. Soofia promised herself that she would try to keep bad thoughts out of her mind and never do anything she knew was wrong. Then she stoned the pillars with all her might and the feelings flowed out of her.

1 *Think of a time when you were tempted to do wrong but resisted the temptation. What helped you resist it?*

Above: Men and women throw small stones, collected at Muzdallifah, at one of the three pillars in Mina. There is a special order and ceremony for this, and it is performed 49 times altogether. Jamrah means "stone" or "landmark": it is the stones thrown at the pillars and the pillars themselves.

Right: Pilgrims crowd round the pillars. The three pillars are named "Greater" (the Makkah end), "Middle", and "Smaller" (the Muzdallifah end).

2 *Add the following to your Hajj word list, with an explanation of what they mean: Hajji, Hajjah, Id-ul-Adha, Jamrah.*

3 *Work with two others. Each of you should retell the story of Soofia's and Karim's Hajj in a different way: (a) as if to Soofia's parents; (b) as if to Soofia's non-Muslim workmates; (c) as if to Soofia's and Karim's children a few years later. Think carefully about what you need to explain and what you can leave out.*

Id-ul-Adha

The hustle and bustle at Mina was to do with Id-ul-Adha, the festival of sacrifice. This celebrates how Ibrahim was willing to sacrifice all he loved most, his son Ismail, when he believed that Allah had commanded him to do so; and how Allah stopped him and gave him a ram to sacrifice instead. The festival reminds Muslims that they must give up everything for Allah. People on Hajj sacrifice a sheep or a goat.

Soofia could not stand the sight of blood, so she was relieved that she didn't have to watch the sheep being killed. There were special butchers in Mina to do this, store the meat, and give it to the poor.

Soofia thought of how Muslims all over the world would be celebrating Id-ul-Adha now, exchanging gifts, giving money to charities, and perhaps sacrificing an animal and sharing the meat. How strange that, at home at Id-ul-Adha, her thoughts had always turned to the pilgrims in Mina, people whom she'd never met; and now here she was in Mina, thinking of her family at home!

Most of the men, including Karim, went to the barber's and afterwards Karim looked just like his cousin's baby when *his* head had been shaved. It was strange for Soofia to see Karim bald, but it also made her think of him as someone who had put his past behind him and was starting his life afresh.

Preparing goats for the Id-ul-Adha sacrifice in a Pakistan market.

Back in Makkah

Soofia and Karim finished their Hajj in Makkah, in the same way as they had started: by making seven circuits round the Ka'aba. It was difficult saying goodbye to the other pilgrims they had met from other countries. They had been through much together.

Some pilgrims were going to Madinah before they left, but Soofia and Karim had been unable to take enough time off work to make this extra visit. They promised themselves that one day they would visit Madinah. They didn't know when – only Allah knows – but they felt sure they would come again.

Some Hajjis and Hajjahs decorate their homes with Hajj scenes, as in this Egyptian village.

Back home

The group went back to Jeddah airport by coach and boarded the plane for home. Soofia and Karim hardly spoke to each other all the way: their hearts were almost too full.

Usually, people returning from Hajj (the men known as Hajji and the women as Hajjah) go straight home. Then their family and friends can visit to hear all about it and show their respects. It is a great honour to be a Hajji or a Hajjah and some Muslims feel that meeting a Hajji or Hajjah brings them some of the blessing of the Hajj, as if they had gone themselves.

Soofia wanted to go to her parents' home straight away. She and her mother hugged and cried together once more. "How's Dad?" Soofia asked cautiously.

"Not too bad, considering ..." her mother replied. "And I'm sure he'll be all the better for seeing you."

4 *In a group, make "Soofia's Hajj Scrapbook" and items to paste in it: e.g. shopping list, postcards, photographs, pressed leaves, some ihram fabric, lock of hair, samples of sand or stone, paper napkins, tickets, vouchers, keepsakes exchanged with other Hajjahs.*

EIGHTEEN

The Qur'an

This unit is about how the Qur'an was revealed and how the book was composed. You will also learn of some important beliefs about the Qur'an.

The Qur'an is the name of the Islamic scriptures. The word "Qur'an" comes from an Arabic word for "reciting". The scriptures are a record of all that was revealed to the Prophet Muhammad, that he was commanded to recite to others. It was during the month of Ramadan, over a period of 23 years, that the Angel Jibril (Gabriel) revealed Allah's message to the Prophet Muhammad (see pages 12-13). Each Ramadan, the Prophet recited what he had been told so far, to make sure that he had memorised it correctly. By the time he died, it had all been written down.

The Prophet Muhammad was not the author of the Qur'an but the mouthpiece through whom Allah chose to speak to all humanity, in the Arabic language. Some passages of the Qur'an are addressed to believers, some to unbelievers, and some to the Prophet Muhammad. The language of the Qur'an has a strong rhythm and is thought to be the most beautiful example of Arabic.

The structure of the Qur'an

The Qur'an is divided into 114 suras (chapters) of different lengths, and each sura has a name – either the first word or the topic of the sura. The Caliph Utman ordered the Qur'an to be composed as one book and the suras were arranged in it in an order that was different from the order in which they were revealed. For example, most Muslim scholars think that Sura 96 in the Qur'an, called "The Clot", was the first to be revealed.

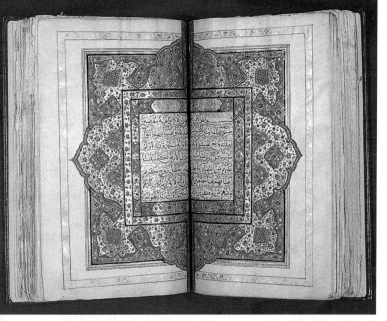

Often a copy of the Qur'an is an object of beauty. Great skill, accuracy, and devotion go into the writing of the words and the making of the book.

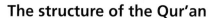

The Prophet Muhammad's First Call
❝ Read in the name of your Lord who creates,
creates man from a clot!
Read, for your Lord is most Generous,
who teaches by means of the pen,
teaches man what he does not know.
However, man is so arrogant,
for he sees himself as self-sufficient,
Yet to your Lord will be the return. ❞
[*Qur'an 96: 1-8*]

The Qur'an opens with "Al-Fatihah", and Muslims recite this at least seventeen times a day, during the five times of salah. The suras that follow Al-Fatihah are to do with laws and the practical matters of running an Islamic community. They were revealed after the hijra, when the Prophet Muhammad was organising the community in Madinah (see pages 14-15). These suras are in a straightforward prose style and are quite long.

The suras later on in the Qur'an are shorter and in a poetic style. They are to do with beliefs and were revealed earlier, when the Prophet Muhammad was still in Makkah.

Al-Fatihah

❝ In the name of Allah, the Most Gracious, Most Merciful.
  Praise be to Allah, Lord of the Worlds,
The Most Gracious, the Most Merciful;
Master of the Day of Judgement.
You alone we worship and You alone we ask for help.
Guide us on **the straight path, the path of those You have favoured,**
Not the path of those who earn Your anger, nor of those who go astray. ❞

Final and complete

Muslims believe that the Qur'an is the final and complete revelation from Allah. They think that the Jewish and Christian scriptures were wrong in places and the Qur'an corrects them. That is why Muslims will not allow any variation on the words of the Qur'an. The Qur'an cannot really be translated without losing some of its meaning. But not all Muslims can read Arabic so there are translations for use in study.

1 ▸ *Summarise the differences between the Makkah suras and the Madinah suras. You could present this in two columns.*

2 ▸ *Read the passage from Sura 96 (on page 38). What suggests this was the first to be revealed?*

3 ▸ *Read both the passages from the Qur'an in this unit. Discuss with a partner what is meant by the phrases that are in bold print. Then sum up in your own words what the passages say about Islamic beliefs.*

❝ I studied classical Arabic at university. It is quite unlike the Arabic spoken in everyday life. After I graduated, I spent a year in Egypt and no one could understand what I was saying at first. I must have sounded as if I was speaking the Qur'an! ❞
[*Liliana*]

In this mosque in Karachi, the mihrab, which Muslims face when they pray (see page 45), doubles as a Qur'an bookcase. The copies of the Qur'an are slipped into their covers before being stacked on the shelves.

NINETEEN

Using the Qur'an

This unit is about how the Qur'an is used and why the Qur'an is important to Muslims.

The Qur'an is the basic source book for Muslims and is a guide for life. Most of it is about what Muslims believe and value. To show their respect for the Qur'an, Muslims treat the book with the greatest care. When they are not reading it, they store it on the top shelf of the bookcase or cover it on its stand. They never handle the Qur'an without performing wudhu, as they do before prayer (see page 21). They must never speak, eat, or smoke when the Qur'an is being read aloud.

1 *Think about the ways that Muslims treat the Qur'an. What does each of them symbolise?*

Learning to read the Qur'an

Most Muslim children attend classes at their mosque or Islamic school to learn to read the Qur'an, and many learn part or all of it by heart. For children the first thing is to *know* the Qur'an completely. Later they learn to *understand* the Qur'an.

Children learn to treat the Qur'an with great care. The boy on the left has the Qur'an on a special cloth on his lap.

2 ▶ *Choose a poem of about ten lines or a piece of prose about 100 words long and learn it by heart. What was easy to remember and what was hard? What do you notice about your memory? Can you still remember the passage ten minutes later? ten hours later? ten days later?*

3 ▶ *Do you agree that you have to know something before you can understand it? Give some examples.*

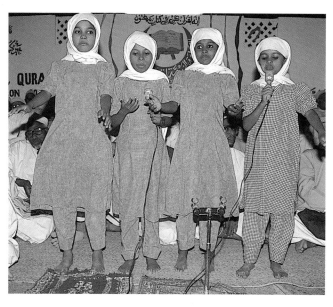

Children at a Qur'an recital competition in Kenya.

Hafiz

Someone who has memorised the whole of the Qur'an has the title "hafiz". In some communities, especially in the Indian sub-continent and among families from that region, becoming hafiz is marked in a special way. The person recites the Qur'an from beginning to end in the presence of his or her family, close friends, and maybe other members of the community. There is often a social gathering afterwards, with a meal, and the new hafiz may be given presents.

4 ▶ *Write a letter to a young Muslim who has just finished memorising the Qur'an. You could write your letter as a greetings card, referring to pictures in this book for ideas for its design.*

5 ▶ *Compose a speech that might be given at a party to celebrate a Muslim becoming hafiz. In your speech, show what you think it means to be a Muslim today.*

Laylat ul-Qadr

During the month of Ramadan many Muslims make an extra effort to read the Qur'an and some manage to read it all. It is divided into 30 readings so that one can be read each day.

A teaching circle in the Al-Azhar mosque, Egypt. There are study groups like this all over the Islamic world, especially at Laylat-ul-Qadr.

Extra prayers are said during the last ten nights of Ramadan and Muslims thank Allah for his guidance. One of these nights is celebrated as Laylat ul-Qadr, the Night of Power (when the Prophet Muhammad received the first revelation of the Qur'an). Some Muslims pray and read the Qur'an throughout this night. In the Qur'an Laylat ul-Qadr is described as "better than a thousand months" and it is said that, on this night, Allah lets the angels come down.

TWENTY

The Sunnah

This unit is about the importance of the Sunnah in Islamic life, the nature of the Hadith, and the use of the Sirah and the Hadith.

The Hadith

As well as the Qur'an, Muslims refer to the Hadith, reports of the sayings of the Prophet Muhammad which were collected after his death. The Hadith are second in authority to the Qur'an. They expand on many of the teachings in the Qur'an and are in an everyday language that is easier for most Arabic speakers to understand and easier to translate accurately. When the Hadith were first recorded, great care was taken to make sure that they could be traced back to words the Prophet actually spoke. Many Muslim customs are based on the Hadith, such as always eating with the right hand as the Prophet told his followers to do.

The Hadith cover all kinds of topics, including prayer, fasting, pilgrimage, government, and law. Those on the page opposite are about social life and human relationships. Several mention "brother", meaning another Muslim or sometimes another human being.

 *Choose one of the Hadith on page 43 and discuss its meaning with a partner or in your group. Express your understanding of the Hadith you choose by creating **either** a picture for which the Hadith is the caption or motif **or** a story or play where the Hadith is the moral or punch-line.*

The Sirah

Muslims also value the Sirah (accounts of the Prophet's life) as an inspiration and a guide to practical matters. Many Muslim customs are based on the Sirah, such as breaking the Ramadan fast with dates. The information about the Prophet and the two stories from his early life on page 13 are from the Sirah.

An Ethiopian Muslim reads quietly and privately from the Hadith.

The Sunnah

The Hadith and the Sirah form the Sunnah. This does not exist as a single book but Muslims see it as the total source of everything known about the Prophet. The largest group of Muslims, the Sunni, are those who accept the Sunnah as the basis of their faith and life.

A selection of Hadith

None of you truly believes until he wishes for his brother what he wishes for himself.

Part of someone's being a good Muslim is his leaving alone that which does not concern him.

He who does not ask Allah for favours, Allah is annoyed with him.

He is not a believer who eats to his fill while his neighbour goes without food.

Every Muslim is the brother of every other Muslim. He neither oppresses him nor forsakes him. He who tries to fulfil the need of the brother, Allah fulfils his need.

A man adopts the way of life according to that of his friend so you should be careful about the one you make your friend.

All the believers are like one man. If his eye hurts, the whole body feels pain and if his head aches the whole body feels pain.

The two Muslims who meet and shake hands with each other are forgiven before they separate.

He who is pleased to see people standing in his honour should seek his seat in hell-fire.

Be in the world as if you are a stranger or a wayfarer.

Powerful is not he who knocks the other down. Powerful is he who controls himself in a fit of anger.

When people see evil but make no effort to change it, Allah will inflict His punishment on all of them.

Teenage girls in school uniform, Jerusalem.

A dealer on the Kuwait stock exchange.

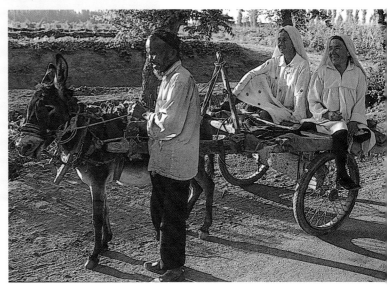

Muslim donkey cart driver and passengers in China.

TWENTY-ONE

Mosques

In this unit you will find out how mosques began, what mosques might look like, and what they contain.

Mosque is the English word for the Arabic "masjid" (place of prostration). It is related to "sujud" (with the same root of letters: s-j-d), which means prostration or bowing down completely. Sujud is the name of the rak'ah in which Muslims prostrate themselves completely, with their head and hands touching their prayer mat. "Sajjadah" (a prayer mat) has the same s-j-d root. Some Muslims are named Sajid or Sajidah.

Buildings

The Prophet Muhammad organised the making of the first mosque when he started the Muslim community in Madinah. These first Muslims built the mosque themselves. It was very simple: the pillars were tree trunks, the walls were of mud bricks, and the roof was of palm branches. But it provided a quiet, cool, clean place for prayer. When the first muezzin called the community to prayer, he stood on the roof and cupped his hand to his mouth to project his voice.

When Islam spread to other countries, mosques were often created by converting churches or other existing buildings. But over the centuries Muslim architects designed and built new mosques to meet the needs of the "jammah", the local Muslim community. Some mosques are grand and elaborate; others are plain and simple. A mosque is usually in the same style as other buildings in the area, but it is always distinctive.

Sometimes Muslims meet for prayer and study in their own homes, or in rented halls, until they can afford their own building.

Mosques in Mali (top), Jeddah, Saudi Arabia (centre), and Malaysia (bottom).

Features of a mosque

All mosques have a mihrab, an alcove or very large plaque on the wall, which shows the qibla (the direction to face for prayer).

Most mosques have a minbar, a platform, where the imam (prayer leader) stands to speak to the people.

There is always a place to wash with clean, running water – outside or inside, depending on the climate.

Outside a mosque there is often a minar (minaret), where the muezzin calls Muslims to prayer. In some communities, the adhan (call to prayer) is broadcast through a loudspeaker. In Britain and other countries where most of the population is not Muslim, the adhan is called from inside.

Rooms in the mosque

Many mosques have a kitchen where food is prepared and served, especially for breaking the fast during Ramadan and at Id (see pages 26-29).

In larger mosques there are madrassahs, rooms or spaces for study, for adults and children.

A mosque may also have a hall for wedding receptions and other social gatherings, a library, and a small shop selling books and artefacts.

Some mosques have their own morgue where the dead are prepared for burial, as this is the responsibility of the jammah.

The prayer hall of the mosque is called the zullah. Before entering the zullah, Muslims take off their shoes and either leave them in a rack outside or take them with them in a bag. There are usually separate areas for men and women to pray. If not, the women pray behind the men. There is no furniture in the zullah as Muslims pray on the floor.

This ornate mihrab in an Algerian mosque makes the qibla unmistakable.

1 ▶ From the descriptions and explanations so far, summarise what a mosque is used for.

2 ▶ Create a general design for a mosque in your area. Think about what it would need to contain, how the qibla would be shown, and how the mosque would look so that it "blended" with the environment but was obviously a mosque.

TWENTY-TWO

The mosque community

In this unit you will see how mosques are used and their value to the jammah (the local Muslim community).

" Prayers in a mosque teach us brotherhood and equality of mankind as in a mosque we find people of all races and classes standing shoulder to shoulder without any distinction of colour, rank, wealth or office. The king may find a labourer standing next to him, a private may be standing next to a general. No worshipper may object to another worshipper standing next to him. All are equal in the House of Allah. "
[Rashid Ahmad Chaudri, *Mosque: its importance in the life of a Muslim*, The London Mosque, 1982]

The jammah should:
- meet for Salat ul-Jumu'ah and hear the khutbah
- make sure that no member of the jammah is in hardship
- provide for Islamic education
- settle any problems or quarrels so that the jammah can be peaceful
- collect zakah (see pages 24-25)
- support each another in any way possible

1 *Think of your class/tutor group as a jammah, a local community. Read what a jammah should do. What should your class/tutor group do or be?*

Putting money in a zakah box.

An Id market inside a British mosque.

In this zullah in Singapore, an address is being given from the minbar.

" Our mosque is more than a place to pray: it's our community centre where we get together at least once a week. Midday on Friday, there's the Salat ul-Jumu'ah, the main event. The imam preaches a khutbah, sermon: he usually talks about something that's been in the news or some topic that might interest us.

Our imam is really good at making links with Islamic teachings. He often refers to something in the life of a Prophet or Caliph. I love it when he retells one of the Hadith (see pages 42-43) and I try to I remember it like a 'thought for the week'. "

[*Fatima Sherif, a family doctor*]

2 *Create a mosque word list by matching these words or phrases with their meanings. They appear in this unit and in Unit Twenty-one.*
Words or phrases: *adhan; imam; jammah; khutbah; masjid; minar (minaret); minbar; mosque; muezzin; qibla; zullah.*
Meanings: *prayer hall; call to prayer; tower for the call to prayer; direction of Makkah; place of prostration (English); prayer leader; local Muslim community; sermon; place of prostration (Arabic); platform for sermons and notices; person who calls Muslims to prayer.*

3 *Imagine that you have the opportunity to speak to a group of people for a few minutes. They are all together, sitting still and keeping quiet. They will listen to everything you say and take it seriously. You have the chance to speak about something that matters to you and which you hope will matter to them. You can probably affect what they think and feel. What do you want to talk about? If you can, write this as a short speech that you could make to a group or your class.*

4 *Imagine that you have visited a mosque and have a postcard with its picture on the front. Write a message for the postcard to send to a friend or relative, saying what you feel about the mosque you have visited.*

slamic art and architecture

This unit is about the characteristics of Islamic art and the beliefs behind it.

1 *What is a pop idol? Do you idolise anyone or anything? What do you think an idol is?*

  66 Say, He is Allah, the One. Allah is Eternal and Absolute. None is born of Him, nor is He born. And there is none like Him. 99
[*Qur'an 112*]

The oneness of Allah

The belief in tawhid – the oneness of Allah – is the most important Islamic belief. Muslims believe that Allah created everything without *being* created, and cannot be compared to anything. This is the heart of the revelation to the Prophet Muhammad and this is why the Prophet was so energetic and single-minded in preaching against idolatry and in clearing the Ka'aba of idols. Idols are limited in size and shape, in colour and texture; they are made and can be broken. No idol – not even all the idols in the world – could ever express the infinity of Allah.

Repeating and interweaving patterns – geometry, calligraphy, and flowery, leafy motifs – in stained glass.

Geometric patterns inside the dome of a mosque in Morocco.

Islamic art is unique in the way that it expresses the glory and the oneness of Allah without using human or animal forms. That is the discipline of Islamic art – what it does not and may not include. But more important is what Islamic art *does* convey. Without the limitations of using figures, Muslim artists express ideas and feelings of infinity through:

▶ calligraphy – beautiful and stylised writing, especially of verses from the Qur'an

▶ geometric designs, especially repeating or tessellating ones that express infinity and reflect the order and precision of Allah's creation

▶ flowery or leafy patterns (known as arabesque), often repeating and set within a definite shape, which evoke a feeling of a luscious garden – of Paradise.

Sometimes artists combine two or all three of these in a single work, and they use all kinds of materials, techniques, and colours.

Among some Muslim carpet-makers there is the tradition of the deliberate mistake – of doing a stitch wrong on purpose. This is because no human creation should ever be perfect: only Allah's creation is perfect.

Some Muslim scholars have drawn links with gardening or farming. They say that when you plant seeds, you first have to clear the ground to prevent weeds and stones from choking the new plants. It is like that with tawhid. Before the belief in one God who has no body can take root, people's minds must be cleared of the idea that there are many gods.

2 *Look closely at the examples of Islamic art on this page and elsewhere in the book. Pick out the use of calligraphy, geometric designs, and flowery or leafy patterns in each example. Discuss what you feel about each piece of art and what it might be saying. Create a panel with the word Islam in it, combining calligraphy, geometric designs, and flowery or leafy patterns. Use the panel as a cover for your Islam file or exercise book, or as the title for a classroom display.*

Painted tiles on the tomb of a 14th-century poet, in Shiraz, Iran. Flowery and leafy shapes are enclosed in a decorative border.

TWENTY-FOUR

Men and women

This unit is about Islamic marriage, and about the roles and responsibilities of men and women.

" It is Allah who made your dwelling homes of rest and quiet for you. "
[Qur'an 16: 80]

Two men and a boy in Jeddah, wearing traditional Saudi Arabian dress.

1 What do you think is the importance of:
- both partners being virgins when they marry?
- both partners being faithful during marriage?
- a Muslim woman marrying only a Muslim man?
- a Muslim man marrying only a Muslim, Christian, or Jewish woman?

2 The Prophet said: "The most detested act out of the lawful acts in the sight of Allah is divorce." What do you think this Hadith means?

Muslims are encouraged to marry and enjoy family life, and the Qur'an says more about this than any other topic. Muslims must not have sexual relations before or outside marriage. A Muslim man may have up to four wives, as long as he can provide and care for them equally, but most Muslim men have only one wife and some say it would really be very difficult to treat more than one wife equally. A Muslim woman may have only one husband. A Muslim man may marry a Muslim, Christian, or Jewish woman. A Muslim woman should marry a Muslim man.

An Islamic wedding is an agreement between a man and woman. The wedding contract is signed by the bridegroom and the bride's male guardian (usually her father) in the presence of two respected Muslim men. The contract usually states a sum of money given by the bridegroom's family. This money remains the wife's property in case of divorce. The wedding ceremony is short and simple, and afterwards there is usually a celebration. In some societies, this is often an elaborate community affair, with feasts and processions.

The wife may keep all the money and property that she had when she married and doesn't have to use it to support herself or her children: this is her husband's responsibility. The wife's main responsibility is to provide an Islamic home for her family. She may take a job and follow her career, as long as it does not interfere with her role at home.

Divorce is allowed in Islam and both partners may re-marry. The process of divorce is quite simple: the man says "I divorce you" three times to his wife, preferably on three separate occasions. Three months must pass after this statement before the divorce actually takes place. This is because, if the wife is pregnant, the couple might not know immediately. The three months also give the couple time, with the help of family and friends, to try to be reunited.

3 *Discuss what Halima says about her family. Do you think she might feel differently if she lived in a society where polygamy (a man having more than one wife) was accepted? List the advantages and disadvantages of polygamy that Halima mentions, for the partners, children, and others. What other advantages and disadvantages can you think of?*

4 *What would be the disadvantages for the partners, the children, and others of a woman having more than one husband?*

5 *Read the two lines from Rumi's poem (below). What do you think he means by "one soul"? Create a picture based on this poem that might appear on a wedding invitation or greetings card.*

" Happy is the moment when we are seated in the palace, thou and I,
With two forms and with two figures but with one soul, thou and I. "
[*Rumi, a 13th-century Persian Muslim poet*]

Halima's father has two wives and Halima's mother is the second of them. Halima says, "I've got two Mums and they're like sisters. My Dad shares his time between them. We live together as one family. I really like it because it's like having an aunty as well as a mother and all us children are like brothers and sisters. Teachers at school get confused about who we are, especially if we talk about our other mother, but we're not confused. My Mum's my Dad's wife in Islam but in British law she doesn't count – and I don't like that. One of my brothers wants to have more than one wife because he can have more children that way – and because the Prophet did. But I wouldn't want that as a wife, because we're not living in the time and place the Prophet lived in. Anyway, I might get jealous and I wouldn't like people thinking I wasn't really my husband's wife."

A woman and her daughters in London, wearing modest, western clothes.

51

TWENTY-FIVE

Parents and children

This unit is about the birth of a baby, and about parents' and children's rights and responsibilities.

1 ▶ *If you became a parent today, what would be the most important thing you would want to say to your new baby? What would your hopes for the baby be?*

2 ▶ *Think about what the man in the photograph might be feeling. Write down what you imagine his thoughts and hopes about the baby's future as a Muslim might be. You could write this as a letter to be given to the child when he or she is older.*

A father whispers the adhan into his new-born baby's ear.

Muslims see a baby as a blessing, a gift from Allah. One way in which many of them express this belief is by making sure that the first sounds a new baby hears are the adhan (the call to prayer) and the ikamah (the call to stand for prayer). Only moments after a baby is born, a family member or friend whispers the adhan and then the ikamah in the baby's left ear. Even though the baby cannot understand what is being said and may not even hear it, the words are an important statement for the family.

The baby's name is announced after about a week. The adhan and ikamah are said again and there is a custom of putting a little honey on the baby's tongue to symbolise the sweetness of the words. Often the baby's hair is shaved and the hair weighed: the family makes a donation to charity of the worth of the weight of the hair in silver. Many Muslim parents name their babies after Prophets, Caliphs, or other important figures in Islamic history. Many others choose a name for its meaning and the qualities that they hope their child will have. For example, the male name Salim means "peaceful" and the female name Imana means "faithful".

The Qur'an does not command parents to have their sons circumcised but most do so, and give hygiene as the main reason. In some societies, a boy is circumcised when he is a baby; in others, he may be several years old. Circumcision is always done before a boy reaches puberty.

Three Hadith about parents and children

Someone asked the Prophet, "Who amongst my near ones has the greatest right over me?"
"Your mother," the Prophet answered.
"Then who?"
"Your mother."
"Then who?"
"Your mother."
"Then who?"
"Your father."

The Prophet said: "Pleasure in the Lord lies in the pleasure of the father and the anger of the Lord lies in the anger of the father."

When the Prophet was asked, "Is there any good I should do for my parents after their death?", he replied, "Yes. You should pray for them, ask for their forgiveness, honour their commitments after them, meet the relatives with whom you have a relationship because of them, and show respect to their friends."

3 In the first of the three Hadith on the left about parents and children, why is the mother mentioned three times before the father? Do you have the same view of mothers and fathers?

4 Some Muslims say that the second of the Hadith quoted means that whatever pleases or displeases a father pleases or displeases Allah. Do you think **this** means that fathers are always right? Do **you** think that fathers are always right?

5 Look at the third Hadith quoted. What is the value of these actions after the parents have died?

6 Write a Parents' Charter based on all three Hadith in the box.

All of Muslim life is marked with prayer. During their lives, Muslims pray for themselves, but when they die – just as when they are born – others pray for them. Here a group of women recite prayers following the death of a woman they know.

TWENTY-SIX

Food, drink, and dress

This unit is about what Muslims may eat and drink, and how Muslims should dress.

1 *Do you "eat anything"? If there are certain foods that you will not eat, what are your reasons? Do you think it's important for people not to eat certain foods because of their religion and culture?*

A Hadith about food

" One never ate any food better than that he got through the labour of both his hands. David, the Prophet of Allah (peace be upon him), used to eat what he earned with both his hands. "

2 *Discuss what the Hadith about food means. Then design a kitchen wall plaque, canteen poster, or something similar, including this Hadith.*

Food and drink

In Islam, permitted things are called "halal". Forbidden things are called "haram". All forms of alcohol are haram. By using a comparison, Muslims consider that all other harmful addictive substances are also haram.

Halal food and drink
- the meat of sheep, goats, cows, and poultry, if the animal has been slaughtered by a butcher who says, "In the name of Allah, Allah is most Great."
- edible plants
- eggs of halal birds (poultry)
- milk from halal mammals
- edible fish

Haram food and drink
- the meat and meat products of pigs
- the meat of any animal which has died naturally or has been strangled
- the meat of carnivorous animals
- alcohol

School girls in Khartoum, wearing hijab (and not covering their faces), as the Prophet Muhammad said.

A Hadith about wine

The Prophet cursed ten kinds of people regarding wine:

66 the one who extracted the juice, who demanded its extraction, who drank it, who carried it, to whom it was carried, who served it, who sold it, who used its income, and its seller and its buyer. 99

Women at the London Central Mosque. Their dress reflects the mosque's international and multicultural membership.

▶ **3** *What harm can alcohol do to an individual? What harm might someone who has drunk too much alcohol do to others? What are the good effects of alcohol?*

▶ **4** *Read and talk about the Hadith about wine. Then make a list of some of the jobs that a Muslim might not be able to do.*

Dress

66 Tell believers to avert their glances and to guard their private parts; that is purer for them . . . Tell believing women to avert their glances and guard their private parts . . . 99
[*Qur'an 24: 30*]

This passage from the Qur'an goes on to say how Muslim women should dress modestly when they are with men who are not close relatives. Most Muslims understand this to mean that women should cover their bodies except for their hands, feet, and faces. But the general rule of modesty applies both to men and to women. Muslim men and women can dress in a style that suits the climate where they live and is in keeping with its culture, as long as what they wear is modest.

In north-west Pakistan, the custom is for women to cover their faces completely when they go out.

▶ **5** *Imagine that you are going to a Muslim celebration and you want to respect the Islamic dress code by dressing modestly. You want to wear your favourite "best" clothes and you cannot buy anything new. Think about how you would adapt your clothing, perhaps borrowing some items. Then sketch your outfit and label each item or feature, saying why you have chosen it.*

▶ **6** *Why is it important for people to dress modestly and not show their body to members of the opposite sex to whom they are not closely related? Is it the same for men and women? Why? Does modest dress stop women becoming "sex objects"?*

TWENTY-SEVEN

Death and burial, and beliefs about the afterlife

In this unit you will learn about Muslim funerals and how Muslims view death and the afterlife.

Muslims believe that death does not destroy their souls, which are taken by an angel to Allah. When a Muslim is dying, friends and relatives stay with him or her, read verses from the Qur'an, and pray that death will be peaceful. The dying person tries to recite the Shahadah: "There is no god but Allah and Muhammad is the Prophet of Allah."

Muslim funerals are always burials. Burial practices show respect for the dead, as well as expressing Islamic beliefs about death and the afterlife. Traditionally, Muslims bury the dead as soon as possible. First, they wash the body thoroughly a few times, beginning with the parts that are always washed before prayer. Then they wrap the body completely in one or more cotton sheets. They carry the body, on a stretcher or in a coffin, to the place where Salatul Janazah (the funeral prayer) is to be said – either a mosque or another clean place. The imam (prayer leader) stands beside the body, facing Makkah, and those who have gathered stand behind the imam, facing the same direction, as they do whenever they pray. Everyone stays standing and says Salatul Janazah in a low voice, as a sign of respect.

1 *Remember a story, play, film, or television programme in which someone has died. How did other characters react? Share this with a partner or within a group.*

These men, in Pakistan, are carrying a woman's body on an open stretcher to her grave. She was aged 40 and died in childbirth.

Part of Salatul Janazah

" O Allah, forgive those of us who are still alive and those who have passed away, those present and those absent, our young and the elderly, the males and the females. O Allah, make the one whom You wish to keep alive from among us live according to Islam and let anyone whom You wish to die from among us die in the state of faith. "

If the dead person is a child, these words are also said:

" O Allah, make him/her our forerunner and make him/her for us a reward and a treasure; make him/her one who will plead for us, and accept his/her pleading. "

Next the body is taken to the burial place. Muslims who see a corpse in procession will stand, out of respect. Quite often, Muslim women do not attend funerals but visit the grave afterwards. In Islamic societies, the body is often placed directly in the ground, without a coffin. The grave is dug so that the body will lie with the head towards Makkah.

The grave is raised a little above the ground. There are no high gravestones or monuments as these are thought to be proud and wasteful. In Islamic societies, mourning may last several weeks and relatives do not attend parties or celebrations during that time.

Life after death

Muslims believe that, when someone dies, his or her soul is taken into the charge of the angel of death. On the Day of Judgement everyone will be raised from the dead to account for their beliefs and actions. People whose good deeds outweigh the bad will go to Paradise. People whose bad deeds are the heavier will be thrown into the Fire of Hell and given hot water to drink and bitter fruit to eat.

2 *What do you think happens to people after they die? If you think that they go to another place or exist in some other way, what do you think it is like? Do you think that the way you see death affects the way you live? Think about this privately or discuss it with a partner. Then express your ideas and feelings in a poem or a picture.*

3 *What do you think this saying of the Prophet Muhammad means? "When a person dies, the angels say: 'What has he sent in advance?' But humans say: 'What has he left behind?'"*

4 *Write a letter of condolence (sympathy, comfort) or design a condolence card for a Muslim who is in mourning. Think about the words and images that will bring comfort and try to express them as helpfully as you can.*

The Garden of Paradise
The Qur'an has many images of Heaven and Hell. In Al-Jannah (Paradise) everyone will be young. It is a beautiful, secluded, green, enclosed garden, with flowering plants and trees. It has four sweetly scented streams, flowing from a fountain. There is no hatred or bad feeling:

66 Where they shall hear no word of vanity; and where there is a bubbling spring 99 [*Qur'an 88: 11-12*].

Salatul Janazah in Granada, Spain. The imam stands in front of the coffin to lead the prayers.

Islamic education

Islamic education

In Britain, most Muslim children and young people go to a non-Islamic school and they maybe attend Qur'an classes in their "free" time. Many Muslim parents would like their children to attend an Islamic school. These are some of the reasons they give:

▶ At an Islamic school, boys and girls are educated separately and this is especially important after puberty.

▶ The children's education can have an Islamic "flavour".

▶ The children would not then have to attend extra "Islam classes" after school.

▶ In Religious Education (RE), the children can learn only about Islam.

▶ The children will be protected from Islamophobia (prejudice against Islam and Muslims), which they might experience in a non-Islamic school.

▶ The children will have Muslim friends.

▶ The children will have Muslim adults as role models.

There are few full-time Islamic schools in Britain and most of them are "private". Parents have to pay fees or the school has to raise funds. For many years the British government refused to allow Islamic state schools. There was a long campaign by Islamic and other groups to have this changed. In January 1998, the British government recognised two Islamic primary schools and agreed that they should receive funds like most other schools. Islamic groups were hopeful that other Islamic schools would also be given recognition and funding.

A teacher and a group of pupils at a private Islamic school for boys, in Britain.

Breaktime at an Islamic day school in Britain which is now state-funded.

1 Draw a chart with three columns and title it "Reasons for Islamic schools in Britain". In the left-hand column, write a shortened version of the first reason listed on page 58 (e.g. "separate education of girls and boys"). In the middle column, explain the thinking behind the reason, based on what you know about Islam (e.g. "important for Muslims to be modest and not to have sexual contact outside marriage"). In the third column, write your views on the reason and the thinking behind it. Do the same for the other reasons listed on page 58.

2 Draft headlines about the news of state recognition and funding for an Islamic school which might appear in a national newspaper (say which one), OR an Islamic community journal, OR the school's newsletter.

3 Working with other pupils, design an Islamic school for a particular age group. Discuss what sort of school you want to create, keeping in mind what you know about Islam and the reasons for Islamic schools. Split the task into particular aspects for pairs or small groups to think about, such as:

These girls and boys are studying the Qur'an together but are seated slightly separately.

- aspects of Islam in National Curriculum subjects
- Religious Education
- assemblies
- wudhu and salah
- clubs and activities
- school dinners
- arrangements for Ramadan, Id-ul-Fitr, and Id-ul-Adha
- school uniform for boys and girls, and staff dress code
- rules or behaviour code

4 Create a booklet of information about the school you have designed. Make the booklet for parents, OR (if your school is a secondary one) for new pupils to read before they start , OR (if your school is a primary one) for children to look at with their parents before they start.

5 Draft a letter to the Secretary of State for Education, asking for the school you have designed to be recognised and funded. What points, questions, or comments might the Secretary of State raise?

TWENTY-NINE

Islam today

This unit is about Islam in the modern world and how it is presented, and about being a Muslim today.

Islam and the news

Islam is in the news almost every day. There may be news items about the actions of governments in Islamic countries, the actions of Muslims who are public figures in Britain today, Muslims in a certain area at school or work, or the relationship between particular Muslim parents and children, or husbands and wives.

Women at a "Rally for Islam" in Trafalgar Square, London.

1 *With a partner or group, take an item about Islam from a newspaper, or from a radio or television news programme. Find out all you can about the background to the story and, if possible, what Muslims think about it. Does the newspaper or programme give just one side of the story? Is Islam presented in a positive or negative way? Can you see any Islamophobia in the writing or pictures? Compare your findings with those of another pair or group who have looked at another story. What conclusions can you draw? For example, are there any "good" stories? How does the way that Islam seems to be presented in the news compare with Islam as you have learned about it? Why do you think this might be?*

The spread of Islam

From the time of the Prophet Muhammad, Islam has spread not only from one generation to the next but from one place to another through Muslims' missionary work. Today Islam is the fastest-growing religion in the world. People are drawn to Islam by meeting and talking with Muslims, by attending events on Islamic subjects, and by articles in the media.

2 *Review everything you have learned about Islam. Then list the reasons why people might become Muslim. Share your list with a partner or group.*

Streaky Sand

Once a woman gave up the religion she'd been brought up in and became an atheist. Later she converted to another faith. Then she became convinced that yet another religion was true and joined that one. Each time she changed, she was certain and sincere, and felt she was making a good move, but those feelings never lasted ... Inside she felt confused and insecure. Finally, she heard of someone who could help her think more clearly and feel more settled. She told him her whole life story and asked him to help but all he said was, "Go home and I'll send you a message."

So she went home and a little glass bottle arrived from him. It was half-full of sand, in three layers – black, red, and white – with a wad of cotton wool to pack it in. The label on the bottle read, "Open the bottle, remove the cotton wool, and shake the bottle. You'll see what you're like." So she did, and the three layers of black, red, and white sand mixed together. She was left with a bottle full of dull grey sand.

[based on a version in Idries Shah, *Thinkers of the East*, Penguin, 1971]

3 ▶ *Read the Muslim folk tale "Streaky Sand" and discuss what it might mean. Then tell the story in one of these ways: (a) as a way of describing what is going on in our society today, as if you were a reporter; (b) as if you were on a soap box, trying to convince people not to change their religion or culture; (c) substituting for "religion" and "faith" anything else which someone might change several times in their life, for example, hair colour, job, house. Does the story have the same meaning?*

4 ▶ *Think over everything you have learned about Islam. What does the "Streaky Sand" story say about the importance of Islam today?*

A speaker at the "Rally for Islam" makes a passionate plea for people to worship the only God, Allah. The banners behind him call on everyone to embrace Islam.

Glossary

Adam   the first man and the first Prophet of Islam

adhan   the call to come to prayer

Al-Fatihah   the opening passage of the Qur'an

Al Jannah   Paradise

Allah   God, in Arabic

Caliph   name for an Islamic leader after the death of the Prophet Muhammad

Hadith   a saying of the Prophet Muhammad

hafiz   a title for a Muslim who has memorised the Qur'an

Hajj   pilgrimage to Makkah

halal   permitted, often referring to food and drink

haram   forbidden, often referring to food and drink

hijra   the flight of the Prophet Muhammad and his companions from Makkah to Madinah

Ibrahim   Abraham, an early Prophet of Islam

Id-ul-Adha   the festival of sacrifice at the end of the Hajj

Id-ul-Fitr   the festival at the end of Ramadan

ikamah   the call to stand for prayer

imam   prayer leader who is often a teacher or religious authority

Ismail   Ishmael, a son of Ibrahim and an early Prophet of Islam

jammah   congregation or local community

Jibril   Gabriel, the angel who communicated the Qur'an to the Prophet Muhammad

Ka'aba   the cuboid building at the heart of Makkah

Khadijah   the wife of the Prophet Muhammad

khutbah   sermon

Laylat-ul-Qadr   the "Night of Power", in Ramadan, when the Prophet Muhammad received the first revelation from Allah

Madinah   the city in Saudi Arabia where the first mosque was built; the second most important city in Islam

Makkah   the birthplace, in Saudi Arabia, of the Prophet Muhammad; the most important city in Islam

mihrab   niche or plaque on a mosque wall, showing the qibla

minar   minaret or tower from which the adhan is called

minbar   pulpit for the khutbah and announcements in a mosque

mosque   place for Muslim prayer, study, and meeting

muezzin   a man who calls Muslims to prayer

Muhammad, the Prophet   the last Prophet of Allah, known as the "Seal of the Prophets"

qibla   direction of the Ka'aba

Qur'an   the Islamic scriptures

rak'ah   prayer movement

Ramadan   Islamic month of fasting

sadaqah   voluntary gift to charity

sajjadah   prayer mat

salah   prayer

salam   peace, in Arabic

Salat ul-Jumu'ah   Friday noon prayers

sawm   fasting

Shahadah   the declaration of faith

Sirah   biography of the Prophet Muhammad

Sunnah   the Sirah and the Hadith

tawhid   oneness, usually referring to Allah

tazbi   beads for reciting the 99 names of Allah

ummah   world-wide Muslim community

zakah   gift to charity which all adult Muslims should give

zullah   prayer hall in a mosque

Index

ANSWERS
Unit 12

The missing words are: Islamic; twenty-nine; thirty; the Qur'an; the Prophet Muhammad; Jibril (the angel Gabriel); sunrise; sunset; eating; drinking; *one of:* it teaches self discipline/it teaches compassion for others/it follows the example of the Prophet; *one of:* pregnant women and nursing mothers/those who are ill or infirm/young children; *one of:* be kind and fair/study the Qur'an/observe their religious duties; Id-ul-Fitr.

Acknowledgements

The author would especially like to thank the following for their friendship and support: Dr Zaki Badawi, Dr Imam Abduljalil Sajid and Sheikh Dr Gamal Solaiman.

The publishers also wish to thank Roy Ahmad Jackson for specialist advice during the preparation of this book.

The author and publishers thank the following for permission to reproduce photographs: Circa Photo Library (W. Holtby): pages 5 centre, 23 top, 25 bottom right; Hutchison Library: pages 19 left, 21 bottom (C. Freire), 22 top (L. Taylor), 42 (S. Errington), 49 left (I. Tree); Christine Osborne Pictures: pages 4 top, 4 bottom, 5 bottom, 8, 14 top, 21 centre, 23 bottom, 32, 34 bottom (Camerapix/MEP), 37 top, 39, 41 bottom, 44 bottom, 49 right, 55, 56, 60, 61; Peter Sanders Photography: front cover, pages 7, 9, 14 bottom left, 15, 19 right, 20, 21 top, 22 bottom, 24, 25 top, 26, 28, 29, 33, 34 top, 36 left, 38, 40, 41 top, 43 top, 44 top, 44 centre, 46 left, 48 left, 50, 51, 52, 54, 57, 58, 59; TRIP: pages 4 centre (V. Kolpakov), 5 top (V. Greaves), 6 (H. Rogers), 12, 14 bottom right (H. Rogers), 25 bottom left (Ibrahim), 27 (D. Clegg), 31, 35, 36 right, 37 bottom (A. Tovy), 43 centre (H. Rogers), 43 bottom (B. Ashe), 45, 46 right (H. Rogers), 47, 48 right (H. Rogers), 53 (Ibrahim).

Artwork was provided by:
Chris Molan pp7, 10, 11, 17, 18; Oxford Illustrators pp 13, 30.

OXFORD
UNIVERSITY PRESS

Great Clarendon Street, Oxford OX2 6DP
Oxford University Press is a department of the University of Oxford. It furthers the University's objective of excellence in research, scholarship, and education by publishing worldwide in

Oxford New York

Auckland Bangkok Buenos Aires Cape Town Chennai Dar es Salaam Delhi Hong Kong Istanbul Karachi Kolkata Kuala Lumpur Madrid Melbourne Mexico City Mumbai Nairobi São Paulo Shanghai Taipei Tokyo Toronto

Oxford is a registered trade mark of Oxford University Press in the UK and in certain other countries

British Library Cataloguing in Publication Data available

ISBN 0 19 917253 6
10 9 8 7 6

Printed in Singapore by KHL PRINTING CO PTE LTD